A Mer

A Memoir

Joyce Kitching

ISBN 978-1-4709-7208-0

First edition
Reprinted with corrections 2012

Grove Publications
81, Grove Hill Road
London SE5 8DF

Front cover: Portrait of Joyce, by Arthur Kitching
Biographical sketch by Stephen Robertson

A Memoir

I first saw the light of day on April 18th 1922. The BBC made a quick note of this, and decided to join me a few months later. It has been a very happy relationship, and we are still the very best of friends.

The venue of my birth was the front bedroom of 20, Bland Lane, Wadsley, in the 4 roomed cottage of my paternal grandparents. Present beside my mother were grandma Bertha Helliwell, and Aunt Ginnie Pulfrey (no relation), our next-door-but-one neighbour, who was the village "sage-femme". She officiated at all births and laid out the dead – a self-styled "hatcher and dispatcher". A rough, loud-mouthed lady, usually attired in a sacking apron and boots, she had no qualifications of any kind, and had learned her midwifery skills at her mother's elbow. Grandfather Fred, a stonemason and builder of stone walls, was boiling the water on the coal fire downstairs. My father, Edwin, would be kept well out of the way of all this and was most likely at work. He was a pioneer motor mechanic apprentice aged 19. My mother Doris was at 21 already adult, and some time previously had been requested to leave her employment as a domestic servant when she was no longer able to hide me under her apron.

20 Bland Lane was the rented cottage of my grandparents, the end one of three, on an unmade road leading from the village to the ganister quarries and the common – a vast area

of heath, woodland, ponds and bogs. It had two bedrooms, and downstairs a living room with a Yorkshire range where all the cooking was done. At the back was a kitchen with a stone sink and cold tap. Outside across a patch of garden was the privy shared with our neighbours the Simpsons, and ultimately used by 9 adults and 2 children!!!

Because of the poverty-stricken state of the young parents, the new family was given shelter from the storm by my grandparents, who, with great generosity, moved their sleeping quarters to the small back bedroom, so that there was room for my cot beside the big bed. 14 months later, we were joined by my brother Dennis, and we were to sleep hugger-mugger in this one room for the next 9 years. I can't remember any other furniture beside beds, but there must have been a cupboard or chest of drawers, for clothes, somewhere.

The living room downstairs had the very basic necessities – a square table with 4 wooden chairs (which I still use), 2 rocking chairs, a large mangle, and a dresser which groaned under the weight of a huge glass case where lived 5 curlews – 2 parents and 3 chicks. The floors were stone slabs covered only with rag rugs which we made in the winter time from old wool-coat clippings.

There were 5 or 6 books – my father's Sunday School prizes, of which I still have 'Blair of Balaclava' and 'The Brave Men of Eyam.' One picture hung over the dresser, painted on the back of glass – a lady in a crinoline standing beside a sort of pagoda. Above the mantelpiece, pride of place, my father's "Sons of Temperance" certificate – framed. An abiding memory is the noise of the merciless draughts playing havoc with the kitchen lino. After dark, paraffin lamps and candles.

Wadsley was an ancient manor, first mentioned in the land tax of 1227. It grew up between the moors bordering on Derbyshire and the city of Sheffield, and is now contained within the city boundary.

It mostly consisted of stone cottages (4 rooms) with slate roofs, built in yards, folds, and small terraces. It had a church, with an adjacent school, Wesleyan Methodist chapel, 3 pubs, village stocks remarkably preserved outside The Star Inn, 3 small shops and a Co-op (our divi number was seared into memory – 6483). One day in about 1926, my great Aunt Ellen opened a chip shop in Water Lane; it was very popular. There was also a Cripples' Home and a very large, behind-high-walls, asylum.

Since the Middle Ages, Wadsley had been an outpost of the Sheffield cutlery trade, and many men still carried on this work in their homes. They were the famous "Little Mesters" – my great grandfather Dennis Inman was of their number, and in a lean-to shed built against his cottage wall, he made pen-knife handles on a foot-operated lathe from which the sparks flew; and it was fascinating to watch. Once a week he took the handles into Sheffield and sold them at the Cutlers' Market. Plying this meagre trade, he had brought up six daughters and a son (who died of diphtheria at the age of 12).

The girls all went into domestic service and then were married to local artisans – Ellen to a carpenter, who used to get roaring drunk (they lived on Cabbage Hill), Alice to a ganger on the railway, Annie to an army sergeant at Sheffield barracks, who was not kind to her, Rose to a baker, Janet never married, and Bertha my grandma was rescued from the shelf at the age of 30 by Fred Helliwell, a widower with 3 teenage sons. My father, their only child, was born in 1902.

So we were surrounded by great aunts and uncles and great grandparents and half cousins for some years, and there was always someone to call on; relatives brought us garden vegetables, fruit, hand-me-down clothes, and village gossip.

The other source of employment was the asylum, surrounded by high walls and secrecy. Both my god-parents, Sally and Harry Shears, were asylum nurses and my mother would have loved a nursing job; there were not enough chores in one small cottage to occupy two women, but the idea was frowned upon. It would have made my father look "unable to provide" – and that would never do. Married women didn't work.

There were no relatives on my mother's side. She had grown up in Gainsborough, Lincolnshire, the youngest child of John and Matilda Dewick. Both her parents died of TB before she was 12, so she was obliged to leave school and be sold into slavery on a Lincolnshire farm. She worked 14 hours a day in winter, and 16 in summer, and grew to loath the countryside. Two years into the war, in 1916, she fled to Sheffield, lived with her older sister Hetty in lodgings, and worked in the steelworks making shells for battleships. She became a city-girl – high heels, smart clothes, lipstick...

But when the war ended, so did the job, and she was back "into service" in Hillsborough. Mr. Fred Hampshire, printer and bookbinder, had gone up in the world. First he acquired a detached house, and then a maid-of-all-work. Finally he bought a car, and when this had to be repaired, it was driven back from the garage by the young mechanic, who would be given a cup of tea in the kitchen. And so it began, walks on the common, rowing on the lake in Hillsborough Park, pie and peas at chapel socials. And then the bitter shame – pregnant and unwed in hostile Methodist territory. It must have been a hard time for my mother – I can't imagine there were any allies.

It was a shot-gun wedding in November 1921, and I arrived the following April. The marriage lasted 45 years – I don't know how. The rows were terrible, when my brother and I would hide under the stairs. They were mostly about money, or the lack of it. I didn't understand for a long time about the gambling, and that we could have left those cramped quarters much sooner had it not been for my father's little folly. It started with greyhounds (the track was near his garage), then motor-bikes, horses and eventually anything that moved. He also chain-smoked. I realised years later how difficult it must have been for my parents – the inevitable tensions of three generations living in four small rooms. In their 45 years of marriage, they had six months at the end, alone, without grandma, and I have come to believe my mother was a martyr. My father now lies between his two women in Addingham chapel-yard. I hope there is peace, at last.

I grew up in a very strict, puritanical family, ruled by grandma, who suffered from obsessive religion of the Methodist persuasion. She went to chapel twice on Sundays, sang in the choir, for some years acted as caretaker, helped to organise the social activities, and saw to it that my brother and I never missed morning and afternoon Sunday School from the age of four. Father always worked Sundays, giving driving lessons, fetching in breakdowns, and I don't think entered a chapel between his wedding and his funeral. Mother pretended to be C of E, but never attended – I'm sure she enjoyed having the house to herself for a few hours. Grandad went off with his cronies on the common – no Methodist he; probably finished up at 'The Cocked Hat'.

The Methodist Ethos was everywhere and we were surrounded by "Thou shalt nots". It was considered very shocking to: -

SWEAR (not even 'damn'), wear flashy clothes and make-up (the epithets were 'tart', 'fast', and 'hussy'), go dancing, or to theatres and cinemas, go to pubs – drink alcohol, anywhere. Play cards, for money, buy things on H.P. Have premarital sex (not spoken about).

To have any occupation other than chapel on Sundays. No knitting, sewing, games, reading (except the Sunday Companion, a dreadful weekly magazine with serial stories in which teachers married vicars and nurses married missionaries, and nobody ever got pregnant outside wedlock).

We had Sunday clothes for best, and weekday clothes, patched and darned, usually second hand, and there was no social life outside the chapel – none whatever.

There were concerts, where everybody had to "do a turn"; "socials", with pie and mushy-pea suppers, where we played games of spinning the plate, tailing the donkey. Concerts, when the choir sang excerpts from oratorios, always parts of the 'Messiah', anniversary sermons out in the fields, Whit

Monday walks, followed by sports, money raising efforts, often for the African mission.

Three bazaars a year. The women and girls produced all kinds of useless articles which were sold to make money for chapel expenses and worthy causes; one year I made 500 paper daffodils, another time hundreds of butterflies, as well as egg cosies, hot water bottle covers, etc.

The African Mission was top of Methodist priorities, and I like to think now that I helped to put Nelson Mandela through Wesley College!

Harvest Festival was a big event in the calendar. After the service we took fruit and vegetables to the workhouse, the Cripples' Home, and the alms houses. Lantern-slide lectures came frequently, usually from returning missionaries. There were garden parties in the summer, and every year from the age of 5 (I think), we signed the Temperance Pledge! Alcohol was the big enemy.

Holidays away from home were unknown, but 3 times in the summer grandma took us on choir "chara" trips to the seaside (Cleethorpes, Skegness and Bridlington). Soggy tomato sandwiches in greaseproof paper, cups of tea from the ubiquitous urn, sand-pies, paddling in cold, very cold, water, red poppies in the cornfields, singing hymns all the way home. The charabancs were very primitive vehicles with soft tops rolled back, until it rained. Then the driver had to stop, get out and pull the hood back over us.

I enjoyed the hymn-singing best. Some of the men had very fine voices, and if I had any ambition then, it was to be a singer. There was no beer on board and we did not stop.

We had NEW clothes every Whitsuntide. My mother made these on her sewing machine. The Whit-Monday Walk was the great annual excitement. Every Sunday School had its own banner, followed by little girls carrying baskets of flowers, the local brass band, all the chapel officials, and children of every age. Traffic was forbidden along the route, and we processed to Hillsborough Park to join all the Methodists of the area, (upwards of 1,500) to sing hymns and praise the Lord as loudly as possible, in order to be heard above the brass. The uniform never varied – straw hat, summer dress, cotton gloves, white ankle socks and white shoes. Little boys wore navy shorts and white shirts, brylcreamed their hair. The ladies re-trimmed last year's hat – a ribbon here, a posy of artificial flowers there – nothing ostentatious. The men wore their one-and-only suit and a bowler. One heat-wave May Day, Maurice Garrett turned up in a boater, and was sent home. He missed the Walk, and arrived later on his bicycle, in disgrace. His was a wonderful baritone, sadly missed.

After "The Sing", we processed back to the chapel, changed clothes, and ran out to the Flanders Field opposite for sports – games, races, potted meat sandwiches, buns and lemonade. My brother and I once won the 3-legged race, and were given an illuminated copy of the 23rd Psalm. Prizes were serious, and came bigger and better for 100% Sunday School attendance. At the age of eight, I received a hardback copy of Mill on the Floss by George Eliot!

My uncle Lawrence was organist and choir-master, and occasionally I was allowed "to have a go" on the harmonium, sitting on his knee while he pedalled – but he had wandering hands, and I didn't like where they wandered, so "no more lessons". We were never warned, as children are now.

Uncle also played the big 2-manual organ in chapel, and we were often required to "pump the bellows". A handle looking like a cricket bat had to be pulled up and down all the time the organ was being played – no air, no sound. And it was not unknown for us to "let the air out" – with dire results; a red-faced organist and a mute instrument.

Everything we used was home-made.

Life was one big cottage industry. My mother and grandma were a very talented pair on the domestic front. Grandma knitted and crocheted continuously. She made the jumpers, gloves, hats, scarves and socks for all the family – always a size too large so that we would "grow into them". Mother had a hand sewing machine and made curtains, dresses, pyjamas, trousers. Winter coats were passed on from cousins and bought in chapel Jumble Sales. These were VERY important. Grandma helped organise them, looked after a stall, and was usually able to manoeuvre the things we wanted to the top of the pile when we arrived. Any woollen garments not sold by the end of the Jumble, could be bought for pennies, and later used to cut into strips to make the rag rugs for the floor. We had a large wooden frame for doing this, and four of us, mother, grandma and children, pegged the pieces into canvas, or sacking, on winter nights.

Grandma taught me how to knit when I was about seven, and mother showed me how to sew a fine seam. The stitches had to be invisible! I learnt to use the sewing machine later, make paper patterns and eventually my own clothes.

Everything was darned and patched. Sheets were turned side to middle, shirt collars reversed. Nothing, but nothing, was wasted, and only discarded when it couldn't accommodate another patch.

The same industry prevailed in the kitchen, where the food was typical peasant and delicious. Bread was baked twice a week, cakes and pies. Jam, chutney, pickles, marmalades made in season; bread and dripping was often breakfast – a hunk of bread and jam after school. We gathered everything that was for free on the common and in the hedgerows – blackberries, rose-hips, bilberries, sloes, crab-apples, mushrooms, elderberries; from the neighbour's farm came milk, delivered from the churn into jugs every morning, the occasional rabbit (which had to be skinned) and sometimes a boiling fowl, which needed to be plucked and "drawn". The feathers were kept to make pillows, and the bones to make soup. I was often allowed to collect eggs at the farm and round the hedges, and I would be given half a dozen to "take to grandma".

Dinners happened around 12.30 and usually consisted of stews, hash, hot pot, cheap cuts of meat, sausages, tripe, poloney, shepherd's pie, offal, and local vegetables. Rice was unheard of except in puddings – which were truly delectable. The milk was full-cream; very unhealthy of course, but made a delicious pudding.

The week had a domestic routine which never varied.
> Sunday. Change underwear and sheets. Bacon and egg breakfast. Chapel. Visits.
> Monday. Wash day. Clothes "poshed" in dolly tubs. My father's greasy overalls scrubbed. Steam everywhere.

Clothes were starched and "blued" and hung out to dry; mangle cranking away all day. A back-breaking business.

Tuesday. Ironing, baking bread and cleaning kitchen.

Wednesday. Cleaning bedrooms.

Thursday. Cleaning brasses, doorstep, with donkey-stone from the rag man.

Friday. Black-leading, Yorkshire range, baking all day. Pies, buns, cakes, scones and bread.

Saturday. Shopping at Co-op.

Friday was bath night. The tin bath was unhooked from the kitchen wall and placed on the hearth in front of the fire, where the kettles were kept on the boil, and hot water was drawn from the Yorkshire range. Both children bathed in the same water; we never saw the bath ritual for the adults. Afterwards, the water had to be ladled out and poured down the sink. The routine every morning was a quick wash in cold water, at the kitchen sink. Teeth were cleaned with a brush and salt.

Our daily needs were well supplied not only by the village shops, but by a diverse assortment of itinerant hawkers, who had their own days and times to arrive on our doorsteps, with their instantly recognisable calls.

Fishy Maggie brought kippers in a basket on Fridays. She had an ear-splitting screech; words never deciphered.

Fishman Bob had fish packed in boxes of ice in his elegant pony-drawn cart, "Coddaneerin, Coddaneerin."

Pot Harry brought pots and pans in a large barrow.

"Wee Willie" staggered around with an enormous case full of underwear, elastic, tapes, cottons, ribbons and pins.

11

Oatcakes, pikelets, tea-cakes, came twice a week, carried in a basket on Danny's head. "Oatepiiiklit".

Billy Bush collected his grocery orders weekly, and always carried in his pockets pairs of spectacles to be tried on.

I don't remember going to Sheffield for any purpose until I was about nine, and then it was for the thrill of a tram ride.

The Church School had been built in 1838 of finest sandstone from the local quarries. A square building with a rectangular bell-tower, it consisted of one large room which could be divided up into two, three, four, classrooms, as and when necessary, by sliding wood-and-glass partitions. The heating was provided by open coal fires and one belching coke stove. It catered for all the village children 5-14 years, and I don't recall any pupil going on to further education.

Outside was a rough, pebbly playground wherein stood The Hut, an ancient black army hut – the haven for P.E. or "drill" in bad weather, for the consumption of packed lunches, and for "noisy lessons" like singing. Over the school wall into the graveyard, which has become quite famous in recent years as the haunt of the young Roy Hattersley, who spent much of his early life in Wadsley – not in a two-up and two-down, but in a modern semi built about 1936. He did not attend the Church School, but travelled daily to a private and more select establishment. The Church School was for the peasantry.

I entered this seat of learning in mid 1927 and a month or so later was sent out into the playground with a piece of smoked glass, all the better to see the total eclipse of the sun. Mother took me the first morning; after that I tagged along with the children from the next yard who were slightly older. Our route lay along Bland Lane, down Coalpit Hill into Pig Street, then Fox Lane, and into the ginnel which led to the church. (Luke Lane was always known as Pig Street because of its malodorous condition.) There was never any traffic (the occasional horse and cart maybe), so we could play games as we came and went – skipping, marbles in the gutter, football, shuttlecocks, hopscotch, whips and tops according to season. My brother and I could call in at "Gran's" (great grandma's) on the way home; she was a great dispenser of iced buns and lemonade, in return for the running of errands – "down to the Co-op, or over to Billy Knott's for a cabbage."

The school had four women teachers and a headmaster, and probably about 200 pupils – two children to a desk with tipping seats and holes for inkwells, (but no ink for the infants). We wrote and drew on wooden-framed slates with crayons and bits of chalk, from day one. Every pupil had a little box of cowrie shells for counting; chanting tables and spellings from the blackboard was de rigueur, and there was a long, long time to go before anybody held the theory that learning should be "fun".

The teacher of the infants' class revelled under the name of Mrs. Woof! (What we did with that moniker can be imagined). She was a round, cuddly, little person with earphone hair-do, frilly blouses, and beads, always beads, every colour and shape and size, and she had a difficulty with her R's. But there was no "play" approach; sums and writing were taken very seriously indeed, a poem to learn every week, and stories of classical heroes. Spellings, spellings and neat script writing.

The incumbent at the time, the Reverend George Cherry Weaver (silver of hair and tweed of jacket) came in three times a week to instruct us in religious matters, and in no time at all, I was a member of the "Ministering Children's League", and wrote its credo in the front of my hymn book:

"No day without a good deed."

"Loving Father make me like the holy child, a ministering child, loving, kind and useful to others. Teach me to feel for the poor and suffering, and may I be ready to do what I can to help all in need." A tall order indeed.

The poor were ever with us. (WE were not poor – not compared.) Morning playtimes found a queue waiting for free cod liver oil – I learnt later these were the children with rickets.

Victor Sage and Leonard Woolley frequently arrived at school with bare feet, and boots given to them by the church ladies quickly disappeared. Pop Shop? The school nurse came in weekly to deal with scabies and impetigo, ringworm and head lice. My mother went through my hair with a small-tooth comb every Friday before the bath – and yes! – there were times ... a quick application of an evil-smelling liquid from a green bottle, rubbed into the scalp, hard, then a towel wrapped round the head – to be slept in. It was felt a shameful experience to be so afflicted, but the little hoppers do not discriminate.

Grandma was very proud of her herbal remedies (we never saw a doctor; in fact there wasn't one in the village. But on the rare occasions when we spied a chauffeur-driven car parked outside a house, we knew there was someone "reight badly" therein.) A doctor had to be paid, and the bills paved the way to the workhouse – ominously situated a mile away.

Aunt Ginnie Pulfrey was the source of Grandma's herbs. She grew these in her patch of garden next to the privy, and sold them for pennies, especially Penny Royal to desperate women. In my innocence I asked, "Why is it called Penny Royal and not Royal Penny?" There was marigold tea for a rash and spots, infusion of comfrey for sprains, yarrow tea for colds, infusion of burdock for ulcers and sores, celandine root for piles, chickweed poultice for inflammation and castor oil for constipation. Ye gods, I remember this one – it took two of them to force-feed me 3 spoonfuls, I was spread-eagled on the hearth-rug, grandma's knee on my chest and her right hand nipping my nose. When I opened my mouth to gasp for air, mother poured it in. There were screams and yells, and Mary Simpson thought I was being beaten to death. No – just violated, for my own good, of course. The winter time brought a great dearth of fresh fruit.

I used to read Grandma's Herbal, looking for alternatives, and the only thing which etched itself in the memory was, "This decoction comforts the heart and drives away melancholy." What was it? I forget. I could have used it many times in years to come. Would it have been efficacious?

But back to school. I really enjoyed it – it was no hardship, and my favourite lessons were reading and singing. And here we must meet Mrs. Hilda Rollins, a lady of formidable mien, straight from the nineteenth century, ram-rod erect, florid of face, wide of bosom, her grey hair scraped up into a flat bun on top of her head. Her manner of dress never varied, winter and summer. She wore a navy blue serge skirt which kissed her black, buttoned boots at the ankle, a high-necked white blouse, full-sleeved, and always at the neck a large, floppy navy blue and white bow. No other adornment beyond a tortoise-shell comb above each ear.

Nobody had ever told Mrs. Rollins that after the war in which she lost her beloved Ted, women had shortened their skirts and shorn their hair. And if they had told her, I doubt if she were listening.

Her impedimenta travelled round with her in a tattered carpet bag. She played no instrument (there was no piano in The Hut), and her entire musical equipment consisted of a tuning fork, a small wooden baton, a modulator and a large bundle of cardboard charts tied at the top with rope. These were hung one at a time over the blackboard. She brought the tuning fork down on the desk, sang a loud top C, and we were away – she pointing to the letters on the modulator, we singing up and down the scale in tones, then semi tones, then intervals, which become ever more complicated. We than sang our way through the charts – which had nothing to do with the popular music of the day but were simple, lovely tunes from the great composers, Brahms' Cradle Song, John Dowland's madrigals, Thomas Arne, Purcell, Haydn, Handel, Schubert, Mozart, Mendelssohn. I could sing "Joy of Heaven" years before I heard of Beethoven. The system Mrs Rollins taught is now credited to Kodaly; we called it tonic-sol-fa, and every choir in the land used it with great success. It was a basic education in song which gave me a life-long passion, and to that austere lady I am eternally grateful.

She had one or two odd little habits. Sometimes at playtime she would produce from her carpet bag a greaseproof paper parcel; one by one she took out raw sausages and ate them with great relish – then licked her fingers, oh, dear!

As married women were not allowed to have teaching jobs, it is most likely that Mrs. Woof and Mrs. Tomlin were also war-widows.

The only man on the staff apart from Mr. Robinson (old Robbo), the headmaster, was Daddy Waite, who taught Standard 4. He had taught my father twenty years earlier, and in every respect he seemed ancient – white-haired, black-suited, with a Hunter watch the size of an omelette pan. He had a disgusting little habit which far out-shone Hilda's raw sausages. There was a coal fire on the outside wall of his classroom. Mr. Waite, perched on his high chair behind his high desk, placidly chewed tobacco (what else could it have been?), and from time to time spat across to the fire. He often missed – there was no sizzle. The fire monitor had the job of going outside for buckets of coal, and at 3.30 cleaning up the hearth. Nobody wanted to be fire monitor.

School days were uneventful; we always walked back home at 12 o'clock for a hot dinner, and by 3.30 we were free; there was no pressure into homework, no feeling that a starry future depended on cramming facts, or that success and money came with exams and tests from the age of seven. There was never the faintest whisper of "scholarships" or secondary school – everybody left school at 14 and went out to work. Fact of life – and eventually got married and had children; we expected nothing beyond.

But living where we did, well away from the city, on a dirt road between two farms – a three minute run to the common, woods, streams, ponds – was a landscape for happiness. We played with the children from the lane and the yard off Coalpit Hill; compared to the deprived children of today, we had incredible freedom – there was no bad man round every comer waiting to steal or harm us. Summer evenings, Saturdays and school holidays were for adventure, imagination – boredom was unknown, the world was our oyster, out of sight of adults, and our amusements cost not a penny. There was a wonderful water-world – damming up streams, sailing boats, making rafts, catching tiddlers, sticklebacks, newts, tadpoles. In the bleak midwinter we slid on frozen ponds, sledged down the steepest hills, and rubbed Jack Frost from the inside of all the cottage windows. I have seen my mother go to make the beds with her gloves on. Chilblains were an accepted winter feature – mumps, measles, chicken pox and whooping cough arrived with the cold weather, so did roasting chestnuts on the open fire, collecting conkers, dragging home logs, bringing in bucketsful of fir-cones and kindling. And the smells of autumn – wet leaves and bracken, mushrooms and toadstools; we knew all the places where the gorgeous, deadly, fly agaric grew, and we were every year warned about that at school. Each spring and summer there was a wild flower competition, so it was no difficulty at all to name names, families, habitats; at this time I developed a great passion for flowers. They grew everywhere, myriads of them, in the fields and lanes, on the common, in the woods. And there was no 'Thou shalt not'. I picked them every time I went out, and arranged them in a long row of jam jars on the coal-place wall, according to colour, – they were my paint box, a palette of ever-changing delight. And I used to WIN the flower competitions, too, every year except one (and SHE cheated!).

Ganister was the yellow silicon rock used for lining the furnaces in Sheffield's steelworks, and was much in demand. It was mined and quarried on the common, and carted off in red lorries which passed our house several times a day. They were slow, and noisy, so posed no danger, games in the lane went on, the drivers waved, and gave us a lift if we wanted one. Several quarries had been out-worked and were derelict, and these were wonderful adventure playgrounds, with rocky valleys for hide-and-seek, mountains of sand, shallow pools of water for floating rafts; as we got older, fires to make from dried heather, gorse, and sticks. Some places were dangerous – I remember scabbed knees, but not a serious accident. Always there were skylarks, curlews and grouse, and one day the shame and misery of treading on a skylark's nest and breaking the eggs. We often found dead birds, and buried them with all due ceremony. From old Harry Pulfrey, Aunt Ginnie's husband, who roamed the common with shot-gun and retriever, we heard tales which always started "When I were a lad," and went on to recount sagas of "derrin' -do," cock-fighting, dog-fighting, bare-fisticuffs; the quarries had witnessed scenes of violence and excitement that we could barely imagine. "Play your mouth-organ, Harry" – and his faithful black spaniel raised her head, closed her eyes, and bayed to the heavens, a dirge, a mournful song, which echoed round the quarry like a banshee wail. Since then, I have never seen a dog so moved by music!

Saturday was different – it was Spending Money Day. We were given twopence each, an absolute fortune, and we ran straight off to Mrs. Bettany's on Pig Street. Hers was a cottage like all the others, but once inside it was truly magical. No stuffed birds on this dresser, but rows and rows of glass jars full of 'spice' (boiled sweets were always 'spice') glass jars on the mantelpiece, on the table, on the floor, but what to choose? You could get four different things for twopence – pear drops, humbugs, aniseed balls, lucky bags, dolly mixtures, palm toffee (Oh! palm toffee, brown and white), and liquorice sticks, telegraph wires, tiger nuts, cinder toffee, spearmint, sherbet, liquorice allsorts, hundreds and thousands, jelly babies, chewing gum, gob-stoppers – it took ages. Mrs. Bettany never hurried us; she sat all in black on her black horsehair sofa and knitted socks on four needles. When we finally left with our booty, we had four little, white-paper bags, cone-shaped, stuffed with delectables. One of mine always contained aniseed balls, because they changed colour as you sucked them – started off red and finished up white, and left your tongue cinnamon-coloured. And you had to keep taking them out to look!

We lived between two farms – Joe Burchenough's at the village end and Harold Stenton's at the common end – so Dennis and I spent a good deal of our time "helping" at busy periods when they needed every bit of labour that could be mustered. Hay making was wonderful – we made haycocks after the hay was turned, and rode on the cart to the stackyard, which always smelt of camomile. Potato picking was back-breaking work even for small people, and it always rained. After the corn was cut, it was the "childer" who did the gleaning. We were paid in kind – eggs, potatoes, cream cheese, cabbages; and at one time I decided I would marry a farmer!

After the harvest, the thresher arrived, wildly pursued by half the village children – up Chapel Hill, round Pond Comer, along Pig Street – to stand in Joe's stackyard like a prehistoric monster waiting for its dinner. With belts clattering and steam hissing, it was fed the sheaves; then magically spat out grain into the waiting sacks and straw into great barrows. The muscle-men who nourished this giant were always friendly – allowed us to sit on the wall and watch, but threatened what would happen if we got down – "We'll throw thi ter t'bull", which was enough to maintain order. Joe kept the only bull in the neighbourhood; we could hear his roars when we were in bed at night, and sometimes watched in utter disbelief as he served his ever-changing harem of Friesian ladies.

Grandad died about the time I started school. He was ill for a long time, an endless time. We were not allowed to make a noise, indoors or out. He grew thinner and bent, and then was unable to speak, even in a whisper. He had cancer of the throat; I don't remember any operation or stay in hospital, but he was nursed with great care by grandmother and my mother. Grandma went into her widow's black, and never forsook it. He was a gentle soul, not given to complaining; I missed him. We would say now that his occupation of stone cutting (without a mask) was a direct cause of his death, but nobody thought of it then. It was long before the days of "chapels of rest", and the body had to stay in the house until the funeral. Before we were whisked off to Aunt Ginnie's, my brother and I were curious witnesses of a small pantomime, and my father's anger, when the bearers were unable to negotiate the bend in the stairs without up-ending the coffin. I don't think we made any connection with grandad at all. Standing at the gate, redolent of Queen Victoria, was the hearse drawn by four black horses draped in black crepe, with long, black plumes on their heads. We were not allowed to watch.

The annual Feast arrived with as much clatter, steam and brouhaha as the thresher; alighted and folded its wings for a week on Baldwin's Field at Pond Comer. Peace absconded.

Traction engines, caravans and wagons stood check by jowl as the fairground men wrought their magic, an overnight marathon, which transformed four acres of pasture into a tinsel-town of light and noise. We were never allowed to go alone, and were limited to three rides. It had the same feeling of excess as Mrs. Bettany's spice shop. Where to start? I feel sorry for today's children who are hurled and thrown about in the name of enjoyment, who have never known the gentle roundabout motion of wooden horses, fiery dragons, and cake-walks (chair-a-planes were whizzy and scary, and not for me). We rolled pennies and threw balls at glued-on coconuts, and always won a goldfish in a jam-jar. One of them lived for five years, and one bitter winter morning was frozen inside a solid block of ice in its bowl on the window bottom – and lived to tell the tale. There were freak shows ("come and see the 6-legged lamb, the wild man from Borneo"), side-shows – always a hang man, and after 1928 a tent showing a 'talkie' film. I usually managed to persuade someone to take me 'round the back' – to see where the real work was being done; the great, powerful steam engines reeking of hot oil, the mechanical music set-up (never to be seen again until the street organs of Amsterdam in '74) and hopefully a peek into the stately homes of the 'travellers' – a plethora of glass-and-brass-and-artificial-flowers. My mother wanted to go into the fortune-teller's tent, but never dared. It was also expensive. Before the days of hot-dogs and pizzas, our culinary delights were sweet – candy floss, barley sugar sticks, bull's-eyes; and the last treat was something to suck on the way home, bought from a strategically-placed stall near the way out. It was a different world, peopled with brown faces that never crossed our path at other times, and bringing an excitement hard to define.

One happy day, gas arrived to Bland Lane – it added a great dimension to our way of life – in fact two. My mother could have a gas ring in the kitchen, as well as gas bracket lights in each room, and outside in the lane, there appeared a green gas lamp, a friend, which was lit at dusk each day by the lamp-lighter Mr. Pashley with his long pole. It meant we could play outside after dark, and games round the gas-lamp, especially swinging from ropes, were a great feature of winter evenings. Initially, there was much disquiet about the safety of all these new appliances; should we be blown up, poisoned by gas leaks while asleep? After a month or two we forgot all about it, and enjoyed the coming of light in abundance. An added bonus was that on ironing day, mother and grandma could heat up the flat-irons on the gas ring, thus speeding up the process, and cutting out coal fires in very hot weather.

I never remember feeling deprived or envious. Nobody of our acquaintance had a bathroom, a parlour, an indoor lavatory, a car. In fact, somewhere around 1924 we had our moment of fame and glory – we were the only family in the village to own a wireless, because my father made one – a primitive crystal set, with earphones, and wires everywhere! The neighbours all came in to hear this miracle of sound – eventually I think, the entire chapel congregation. We were never to be without a wireless – the next one ran from a wet battery which had to be recharged every week, and woe betide you if the acid spilled on to your shoes.

My father was a born craftsman with a great flair for invention. Engines of any kind were his pride and joy. Had he come from a family which recognised his talents, and been able to give him an education beyond fourteen years, I'm sure he would have become a successful engineer. But he loved motor cars, the look of them, the sound of them. He could "tune" an engine until it purred for him, and no problem was ever without solution. But life took him by the scruff of the neck. By the age of 21, his apprenticeship finished, he had a wife, two children and his own tiny business in a shed in Hillsborough, an outer suburb of the city. We hardly ever saw him; he worked seven days a week all his life – or he was away from home seven days a week, and Sunday was his busiest day, to grandma's great chagrin. Cars were not numerous in the decade after the war (you had to be well-heeled), but if you owned one, then it had to be taken "for a run" on Sundays – indulge the family, let the neighbours see. And they broke down, or crashed. My father, single-handedly, ran the local lifeboat service – he was captain and crew, and I don't think he was ever happier than when towing in the casualties to his little harbour yard. Sunday was a red-letter, wreck-littered day, and provided work for all the ensuing week. Dennis and I took his Sunday dinner for him, between two plates, packed with towels, in a large basket. "Walk as fast as you can, and don't shake things about or you'll spill the custard." And whilst he was eating, in his cupboard of an office, we explored the contents of the yard – the torn leather and battered chrome, twisted bumpers, broken seats, shattered windscreens (often with splatters of blood), blown tyres, squashed bonnets, some a complete write-off, some worthy of serious surgery and intensive care. My father was the man. My brother couldn't wait to get his hands on a steering wheel; it put me off wanting to drive for the rest of my life.

When one of his customers was knocked down and seriously injured crossing the road, my father embarked on his magnum opus – his great invention for saving life. It involved an extra bumper on the front of the car; this contained an intricately folded aluminium and canvas bag; at the press of a button, I think on the dashboard, this opened in a split second to scoop up the pedestrian, ensuring minimal or no injury. At first, it was a failure, but refinement followed refinement, the materials used became lighter and folded into less space. After about four years of trial and error, it was ready. My father stepped off the pavement in front of a car driven by a friend, travelling at 30 mph, everything worked perfectly, and he suffered not a scratch. Jungle telegraph spread the good news and the Sheffield Telegraph appeared on the doorstep, and some months later we were taken to the Hillsborough Kinema to see Dad on the silver screen in Pathé Gazette repeat the performance.

The word 'fortune' was bandied about. I think my mother had visions of a rosy future – it was going to completely change our lives. And of course, it did nothing of the kind. It was hawked round from one car manufacturer to another, and rejected at every turn, the main reason given – that an extra bumper would spoil the LOOK OF THE CAR! So no, thankyou. Nobody was the least bit interested in preserving the life and limb of pedestrians. Things have not changed. My father, a bitterly disappointed man, wrapped it in a tarpaulin and stacked it in a comer of the garage, where we found it, covered in dust, after he died in 1966.

When I was ten, he did something quite unheard of for a young man in the village. He upped and left it – gathered his mate, his brood and widowed mother, and migrated to Stannington, a village on the other side of the Loxley Valley about five miles away, to live in a burgeoning shanty town on the steep hill only 200 yards outside the city boundary (a fact which made for trouble later). We were still in the country, but only a one-and-a-half mile walk through fields, to the tram terminus. In the golden days before the planners arrived, a man could build himself a nest, no matter how bizarre, and feather it to his heart's content, without let or hindrance. This particular nest had been built by one old bird Reg Rightam, and feathered by his son, from a collection of bricks, concrete and pebble dash.

They had grown weary, or run out of money, and never finished it. A bungalow on a quarter of an acre of wilderness, it had a living-kitchen with Yorkshire range, sink and built-in copper, three bedrooms, a half-finished bathroom, and a small, dark, front room. Lit by gas, it seemed, and indeed was, enormous after grandma's cottage. The miracle was that my father had been able get a mortgage on it! Our neighbours lived in the most outrageous collection of dwellings imaginable – caravans, army huts, corrugated iron sheds, loosely scattered around a dirt road leading to the village. Across the road (a great stroke of luck), Wragg's farm, where lived two children the same age as Dennis and me, and we were very quick to fraternise. Our nearest neighbour, Percy Chadwick, was a joiner, building himself a wooden house with a verandah and greenhouse. POSH.

Stannington had no ancient connections or trades, and its houses, none older than a hundred years, were not built in yards and folds, but either side of a main street which started at the Sportsman Inn and wound uphill for three quarters of a mile to the post office, elementary school, chapel and church. There were recently-built semis and a few council houses, two or three pubs, and the main centre of employment, two enormous brickyards, which made bricks for housing and Sheffield's steelworks. No sign here of the famous cutlery trade, no cottage industries.

Gardening was not my father's cup of tea, nor my mother's. But grandma, already past 60, took to the quarter of an acre jungle like an Irish navvy. From a previous life it had two apple trees and hundreds of raspberry canes; before long, there were vegetable and herb patches the envy of the colony, a primitive lawn and a rose-bed. My father underwent a startling change of character too. Suddenly, he became a man of property, fancied himself a farmer, bought a shot-gun, a rifle, three ferrets and a spaniel retriever called Simon. On his rare half-days off-duty, courtesy of the local land-owners, he went shooting rabbits. We ate rabbits until the sight of them brought on panic attacks, and sold the surplus for 6d each to neighbours. We saw no more of him than before the move, if as much.

About this time, Dennis and I went our separate ways. He found football, and rough friends who did barbaric things to small animals. I joined the Brownies at our new Methodist chapel, which was bigger and more opulent than Wadsley's, but still had an outside privy. We missed the common and the quarries, but Rock Wood, very aptly named, was just beyond the garden wall, a precipitous descent to the River Loxley and the fields beyond. One of the worst disasters of Victoria's reign occurred in this valley in 1864, when the Dale Dyke Dam, at its head, nearing completion, burst its banks in a night of terrible gales. The flood of icy water rushed the eight miles into Sheffield, and beyond, destroying everything in its path, and killing 250 people before dawn broke.

No warning reached the villages down the valley. Houses, factories, shops, bridges and mills were destroyed, their occupants drowned, or killed by the mass of boulders, trees, machinery and wreckage that swept from the hills into the poorest districts of Sheffield and on as far as Doncaster. This happened eight years before grandma was born, but she told us stories about it as her parents remembered it; how relatives and friends became unemployed for years – others had to leave the village to find work, and how the pattern of working life there was permanently altered. Whole families died, farms never recovered, and the flood cast a blight on the valley for the next fifty years.

Grandma suffered most from the move to Stannington. She had grown up and lived in the same small area for sixty years – she missed her friends, her relatives, and most of all the chapel. She never took to the new one – didn't like the people, and always in the summertime she walked back to

Wadsley on Sundays, through the wood and down the valley, a return trip of about six miles. I think this is why she addressed the marathon task of the garden with such vigour. It was a solace. But mother made friends. She volunteered to help on two afternoons a week at the village baby clinic, weighing babies, keeping records – in her element; and she got to know the district nurse, the health visitor, and the other volunteers, one of whom was Miss Lomas, daughter of the only top-drawer family in the area. Her father was managing director (owner?) of Lomas' brickyard.

Mother's sewing machine went into overdrive (the only things she couldn't make were stockings and shoes), and when she sallied forth to her clinical duties, she looked every inch the lady. She came to know all the young mothers in the village, and sure enough, still only 32, she was just a young mother herself. She was a beautiful woman, with lovely hair and finely chiselled features, and she could WEAR HATS. Whatever thing she put on her head looked terrific; she could have worn a lampshade and gone out with confidence. Father's business acumen began to show favourable results, because he took on a 14-year-old boy as apprentice; the arrival of Douglas meant that he could take off the occasional few hours to "go out with the guns", and bring home more rabbits!!!

We were no longer living in grandma's house, but she still ruled the roost. Occasionally, mother would make a bid for power, usually on the furniture front. Gradually, she threw out the old dresser, the rocking chairs, and substituted them with modem veneered tat "bought" with coupons from Ardath cigarettes. One chair cost 3,000 coupons! The more you smoke the cosier you are.... Father was warned at the age of 60 that smoking would be the death of him, and four years later, it was.

The bungalow's three bedrooms were apportioned as expected; parents in the largest, brother Dennis in the smallest, and grandma and myself in the medium one. Apart from two years, during the war, I was to have a bed in grandma's room until the night before I was married. We were still without electricity, and all the appliances that go with it, but we were the grand owners of a bathroom and an indoors lavatory. Bliss. Dennis and I had never encountered the blessings of the city. We knew nothing of libraries, art galleries, swimming pools, theatres, cinemas, concert halls, restaurants – but we knew a VERY great deal about the countryside. I am at home there, I suffocate in the city.

I became a loner – Simon the retriever was my passport to freedom, my licence to roam, and I was allowed to go anywhere in his company.

We jumped the garden wall, ran down the lane into the wood, and were away. He was the most amenable creature on four legs, wouldn't hurt a fly, a burglar, or a villain of any sort – his job was to bring in the dead rabbits; but he was my guard-dog, and I thanked my lucky stars that my father had taken up hunting. We found new woods with pheasants and bluebells, a patch of rare spotted orchids, sad ruins of water wheels and mills left by the flood, and never another lone child.

Dennis and I transferred quite painlessly to the new village amenities. Grandma was a newcomer to the chapel – no longer kingpin, she was involved with very little, so no more 'socials', bazaars (Hallelujah!) – we were outside the Whitsun Walk territory, nobody set up sports and games, and our only obligations were morning and afternoon Sunday Schools.

These sessions were conducted by two Superintendents, one of whom had a speech impediment so awful we understood about one word in five (I think he had no roof to his mouth). The other abused the English language in a dialect so impenetrable, it was foreign even to our Yorkshire ears. (His job was to take round the night-cart emptying the middens.) They were both bible-thumpers, zealous and sincere, and neither of them should have been encouraged or allowed to indulge in an occupation which needed communication skills to the young. There was a Brownie pack, and a Guide company, but I was disappointed to discover there were no 100% attendance prizes, and no choir trips to the sea-side. Or if there were, grandma wasn't interested, and we didn't have sand between our toes for a long time.

The village had two centres of education – the old one was church endowed, and stood at the very top of the main street. Ours, the elementary school, neighbour to the chapel, was much bigger, of recent vintage, and boasted a fine asphalt yard with loos where you pulled a chain. It had a large, central hall, surrounded by about six classrooms, and again catered for all children 5 – 14 years. At 14, you left to get a job – the boys mostly at the brickyards, and the girls in shops and offices in Sheffield's suburbs. The staff consisted of five women, three war widows and two unwed ladies, and Mr. Albert Heeley, the Headmaster, an erect, grey-faced war veteran, ex-officer, with a shattered right hand and a shell-shocked head. He was the essence of kindness and courtesy until provoked, and then, he had a terrible, uncontrollable rage, which we always knew was coming to the boil when he shouted 'Shut those windows.' He rampaged round the school, thwacking his cane at anything in his path, incoherent and very loudly possessed. But he was a sad and contrite man when the choler had passed – sat with his head in his hands, and his body shook. My teacher, Mrs. Hague, explained what shell-shock was, and that we should be sorry for him. And we were – and still frightened.

At Christmas, mother's social life became a many-splendoured thing, and there was much excitement. She was invited, along with all the clinic ladies, to take tea with Miss Flora (Lomas), at the Grange, and that was the first time in her life she had been served a cup of tea and cakes by a maid in uniform – "made a fuss of' as she called it. She went to the hair-dresser's, a luxury unheard of, and when grandma had gone to the farm to fetch eggs, she inexpertly applied the lipstick and rouge, slipped into the high heels, and fled. The icing on the cake was being transported to and from the clinic in a chauffeur-driven Bentley, an experience which glowed for weeks, gave off a very comforting radiance. She had a live-in babysitter, but hardly ever went out. Years later, when I was far too old to be called "a cheeky madam," I rebuked my father for this. He could have done better; if he had cut down the smoking a bit, he could have afforded it. There were no stairs to hide under now, and when the rows became explosive, Dennis and I repaired to an old wooden shed in the garden, where he reared beautiful, white fan-tail pigeons, and father kept his ferrets. We were forbidden to open the cage door – "ferrets can bite your fingers off".

Stannington had fewer hawkers and more shops – a complex round the school of post-office-cum-grocer-cum-baker, a butcher's, a hardware shop where you could buy wire-netting, clothes poshers and dustbins, washing lines, paraffin lamps and paraffin. (Our bungalow had gas, so we were greatly blessed.) Fruit and vegetables arrived twice a week on a pony-drawn cart. The great surprise was the forge – the blacksmith's shop, across the road from the post office. We had never seen horses being shod before – the red hot fire and bellows, sparks flying, the horrible, acrid smell of burning hair and hoof – patient Shire horses standing immobile, never running away, and Marjorie's Dad hammering on the new metal shoes. One day as we stood watching, she came out of the forge cottage and addressed the little gathering, "Who'd like to come and see mi grandad?" We followed her indoors, and there, in the middle of the living room on a trestle table, was grandad in his coffin.

The next summer I discovered I had a taste for composition. Mr. Heeley's nature was highly competitive, and one of his basic tenets was that competitions were good for the soul – there was always a competition of some sort happening in the school, and he was usually at the helm – Wild Flowers in Spring and Summer, impeccable hand-writing, at all seasons, home made models, knitting, wood-work, you name it. One morning in assembly he announced a story-writing competition and as I listened to Children's Hour on the wireless and had just heard Auntie Muriel talking about Robinson Crusoe, I decided to enter. From what I gathered later, it was not exactly the authentic version – but it won a prize, something like three big packets of seeds for my school-garden plot. (Adjacent to the school was a field which had,

33

over the years, been cultivated by Albert and his minions, and transformed each summer into a blaze of glory.) It also resulted in a letter to my parents suggesting that I take the II-plus exam the following February. There was general bewilderment – what was that all about? None of us knew of anybody who had stayed at school beyond the age of fourteen. There was humming and ha-ing; would it mean school uniforms and bus fares? I think the question must have been well-aired at the baby clinic, because somebody (Miss Flora?) told mother that it could mean a good job at the Town Hall, and that appealed greatly to mother's general sense of direction. She went to see Mr. Heeley, and agreed; and we forgot all about it.

Christmas came and went, unremarked; by the end of the first week in January, childhood was over. No warning. Finished; I was not consulted. It did not leave with my benediction. I was not very well – childish tummy upset, some pains, some sickness. In those days, it was called a "bilious attack", better next day. But this one wasn't – two days, three; regular dosings of grandma's herbal concoctions, which were returned to sender, no delay. On the fourth day, even I knew that something was badly wrong. Have you ever heard of anybody whose life was saved by a piccalilli recipe? Don't go away, you will. In the evening, one of mother's clinic friends, a little Irish nurse called Nurse Lawlor, propped her bike against the hedge, and came in for afore mentioned recipe, promised the previous week. She was ushered in to have a look at the child; pulled up my nightie, took my pulse, and with a cry of "God Almighty" (very unprofessional), ran out of the house to the farm across the road to use the telephone. After that things happened pretty fast. There was a bumpy ambulance ride down the lane and across the northern deserts of Sheffield to the City General, washings and shaving, and a hazy voice telling me to count. At midnight, the gentle Scottish Surgeon, James Clarke, told my mother, "We have done our best for this little girl, but it is quite possible she will not survive the night." An opinion not reported to me for some years. But as we all know, this little girl DID survive the night, and thousands of subsequent nights.

I woke into a woozy world next morning to find a large, bespectacled face bending over me, and a very concerned voice saying, "Poor little bugger". When I surfaced enough to look around, I realised I had been misinformed. Mother told me in the ambulance that when I woke up I'd be in a large room with lots of children. Not a child in sight. I was in a large room, much later described as a Florence Nightingale ward with 24 beds, whose occupants were lying down, sitting up, or perched, and they were all women! One by one, the perchers, the walking wounded, came to inspect the new resident. And very welcoming they were, too. "Don't worry, luv. You'll be all right. We'll keep an eye on you. Don't worry now." And I was in no state to worry, or do anything else. I was in the comer bed, next to the door and the nurse's office – on reflection some time later, the best possible position for a hasty, unobserved exit; no one would notice, or be upset.

That evening, both my parents came to visit, so I knew this was something special, I had never been away from home before, helpless among strangers, not knowing what on earth had happened to me, and very frightened. The woman in the next bed was very ill, and hardly ever opened her eyes, or spoke to me. She died two nights later; I couldn't see, but I

could hear her incoherent ramblings, her cries of distress –
she wanted Tom, son? husband? Nobody came. Then silence.

The night-porter came with his trolley and took her away,
quietly, efficiently. I wondered where to... We were wakened
at 6am for breakfast, but I was on drinks only out of cups with
little spouts. The walking wounded used to come and perch
on my bed – a bit of banter; but I couldn't return it, weak as a
kitten, as they say. When the dressings trolley came round
every morning, no concession was made to my tender years.
With one exception, the nurses were very kind, but they did
what they had to do, and if I yelled, which I did, sympathy was
in short supply. But the perching ladies made a rough-and-
ready rota to come and hold my hand, and they left toffees
which I could not eat lying flat.

One day oozed into another; I began to notice the daily
rituals, the pecking orders, who did what, when – a doctor
was a doctor, but a surgeon was a Mr. – very odd. The
youngest nurses had the filthiest jobs; how did they keep
those silly hats on? Matron sailed in, with a fanfare of
trumpets, and Dr Cochrane, the young houseman with curly
hair, had film star status. The jokes and innuendoes flew over
my head; I was excluded from the badinage – hadn't a clue
what was going on.

There was much pain and sorrow on the ward – during the
day camouflaged by busy-busy, comings and goings, visitors
some evenings (how things have changed). During the night
there was no escaping it, bleak and raw, I was terrified.
Fingers stuffed in ears, head under the bed-clothes till gasping
for air, I was alone, abandoned and afraid. Nobody would tell

me why I was in a vast room full of suffering women; I pleaded to go to the children's ward; my pleas went unheeded.

All I could see of the great outside world was a tiny patch of sky. The windows were high, sash, and always open at the top. (How things have changed.) One afternoon I lay and watched snow drifting in and settling on the bottom of the bed; the window was eventually closed. For two or three days, I asked so many questions (was it still falling, how deep was it? were the buses stuck?) that two ministering angels propelled my bed out onto a little verandah, piled on the blankets and left me to say hello to the world. It was as beautiful as I remembered it – steely grey and blue sky, and deep snow with purple shadows, I could hear children sledging beyond the hospital grounds, and the buses chuntering up the hill to Five Arches. What I would have given to be out there – but it was back to Miss Nightingale, and the grown-ups. Most patients went home two weeks after surgery, but not the child. Four weeks, five, on and on, the days were endless, but once able to sit up, I begged for things to do, and the nurses obliged. I made hundreds of cotton wool swabs, folded endless bandages, mended slings, and then I started reading, anything, women's magazines that were passed round, newspapers, books from the library trolley, which were always romantic stories of beautiful girls, handsome men and a no-good cad – nothing at all suitable for my age. T.V. had not been invented and wireless sets were enormous, non-portable, so I don't remember any music at all; there was much card playing among the walking wounded, and one afternoon a lovely woman called Dorothy taught me how to play patience. Full of enthusiasm, I wrote home for a pack of cards, waited, and waited, but it never arrived. When my mother visited on Saturday, I told her the cards hadn't come, and she said "No, we thought best not. We don't want you playing cards on Sundays." And for the first time, I think, I felt the cruel injustice of life – a crack appeared on the earth's surface, a tiny fissure which over the next four or five years became a yawing chasm. I began to question the rules laid down for me; there were so many of them, some without rhyme or reason, and in very small ways, I began to rebel, even so young.

One night, as Mrs. Maskery was dying two beds away, the idea came to me (why had I never realised it before?) that I was in the Dying Comer, next to the door, and the nurses' office. THAT's why I was there; it was going to be MY turn. I kept myself awake, and next day began another campaign to be moved to the children's ward. I was inconsolable; nobody would listen. I was told not to be a silly girl, but the terror never left me. I knew about the alone-ness of life at the age of eleven, so that when I was obliged to live alone twenty years ago, I was probably more prepared for it than most people. Women came into the ward, recovered (or not), and went home. They were the wives and daughters of steel-workers, miners (one of my ward-mates had a husband who was a tram driver) – and I never in all that long time heard one B.B.C. accent; rough diamonds if you like, but they adopted me, I was their "little lass", something of a curiosity, because their own children, if they were under twelve, were not allowed to visit; I thought it very unjust.

One memorable morning at the end of his round, Mr. James Clarke, surgeon, came and sat on my bed. "What do you say to the idea of going home?" "Oh, yes please," I said, remembering grandad, "I'd much rather die at home than in here." He seemed a mite perplexed that I should be considering such a thing. "You're not going to DIE," he said, "you're our miracle girl. You're going to get better; write and ask your mother to fetch you Saturday."

And I did. Forty six years later, when I was sifting my mother's bureau the week after she died, I found this letter, written in pencil in impeccable script; it finished "Please don't be late." And she wasn't. My father came, too, in the latest car he had knitted from a wrecked Austin and a Standard; it had a hard top, and room for three people to sit side by side. I'd had two days to practise walking. Foot had not met floor for nine weeks (how things have changed), and all leg muscles had emigrated. So I was wheeled out by my two favourite nurses and lifted into the car. I couldn't believe it; they both very unprofessionally kissed me goodbye, the child in the comer who had become part of the furniture. I never saw James Clarke again, but his face I have not forgotten; a little Irish nurse and a shy Scottish surgeon gave me (up to now) sixty eight years of glorious life, and because, at a very impressionable age, I saw, and understood, the alternative, every day has been precious, enjoyed to the limit, and thankfully appreciated. What a gift – and they never knew.

It was quite a homecoming. My brother had not seen me for nine weeks – he was too young to visit, and he seemed genuinely pleased I was home. The neighbours came with lIttle offerings, and class-mates brought news of school. It was altogether too exciting, and I was carried to bed; my favourite tea came on a tray – boiled onions in cheese sauce and scones and strawberry jam. Bliss!

Grandma's bedroom was very quiet after Ward 12, but I quite appreciated the lack of drama, especially at night. Simon leapt in, expecting long walks, but it was to be all of six months before I could stand erect and walk any distance.

Although relieved and happy that I was returned to the fold, mother and grandma were deeply shocked at the turn my education had taken, because I knew all about swear words, bad ones, dropped wombs, pox, hysterectomies, white legs, breast cancer, epileptic fits, and why some women's skin turned black and they died a horrible death because they didn't want babies (how a botched abortion was explained to a child). Nurse Lawlor came and drew me diagrams – told me what had happened. It was peritonitis, a ruptured appendix, "very dangerous, love." And I have learned since that indeed it was; money was no help – the rich and famous were not spared (Rudolph Valentino died at the age of 29) – until the discovery of penicillin. All glory be to Alexander Fleming,

I managed to unhook grandma's mirror from the top of the drawers, and the first sight of my lopsided little body was one of life's traumatic moments. South of the navel closely resembled a road-map, with added deep pot-holes where the tubes had been, and as a scar, like a diamond, is forever, I knew I had to accept this unlovely thing, but nobody was going to see it, NOBODY, NOT EVER. Mother and grandma already had, but nobody else, ever, not ever.

There were not many physiotherapists in those days, and progress to recovery was slow. I'd missed the scholarship exam, of course – but it didn't seem important. I'd had a DIFFERENT education, shaken hands with terror, waved off the Reaper, lived on the battlefield, and I came to know, long before I could put it into words, that there is NO WEALTH BUT LIFE. This was the time that shaped me, gave me attitudes I still recognise; I'm a survivor. And every day, the world is as miraculous as it looked that morning I was wheeled on to the hospital verandah to see the snow.

About this time, some government edict decreed that country villages should enjoy the benefits of a public library; the one that came our way was on wheels, a book-lined van every Wednesday, driven there by an obliging young man who seemed to love his job. There was a great preponderance of crime and detective novels, but I'd read anything – Edgar Wallace, Rider Haggard, school tales: I was omnivorous. The Library Van was the second life-saver that incredible year. There was a third. I had an imminent birthday, and THIS year, I was asked if there was anything **I'd** like. (Usually it was something to wear – a grandma jumper.) THIS year I was ASKED,. And I heard a small voice say, "I WOULD like a piano, if that's alright?" A piano? Well, we DID have a front room with no furniture in it, and there seemed no harm in asking; not much hope, really. But one night after dark, a piano arrived, on a lorry, to my utter astonishment and delight. It was yellow of key and squeaky of pedal, its candlesticks had been removed, but there it stood, in the otherwise empty front room, just waiting, grinning – and I had all the time in the world. I was never told its origins – probably thrown out by some relative, but we took to each other from the moment of introduction, and began a liaison which has endured to this day.

There were a great many discoveries to make. All I knew about a piano was that it had black notes and white notes, and that wasn't much help. So I borrowed grandma's Sankey and Moody (which I could sing from cover to cover) and tried to work out the lines and shapes, with no success whatever. And then, I spied the tonic sol fa, and we were away, every tune, one finger, always on the white notes. I could make sense of the beast, at a very primitive level; it was fantastic. Every afternoon we listened to Children's Hour on the wireless, and after that, whilst we were eating tea (high tea), mother had on her favourite programme the Big Dance Band, which for a long time was Henry Hall, with Les Allen and Kitty Masters, crooners. The tunes were easy, and we loved them. After a couple of listenings, I could play them, all in the key C, and I think I drove the family to distraction, only coming to a halt when I turned blue with cold. The one coal fire was in the living room, and a second fire was an incredible rare luxury, reserved for Christmas, special visitors, and sometimes Sundays.

After that, it was but a few more experiments to chords and harmony, and I could never have arrived there without Mrs. Rollins and her modulator in the scruffy army hut next to Wadsley churchyard. My burning ambition was to play like Charlie Kunz, syncopation and pop songs – these, and hymns, kept me busy for months.

By the time summer arrived, my legs had begun to understand their function in life; no running, jumping, or climbing, but that worried me not at all. Walking was fine, the woods and the river still beckoned, and my guard-dog never declined an excursion. And then, great excitement, I had a whole week's holiday at the sea-side. Grandma's sister Janet (the one who never married) earned her living as a maid-of-all-work in a Blackpool boarding house on the sea front, and I was to be allowed to stay with her on some kind of arrangement with her employer. I slept on a camp bed in Aunt Janet's room, which was an attic at the top of the house, not much bigger than the linen cupboard, and ate with her in the kitchen when all the guests had finished their meal. I helped with little jobs like clearing tables and washing up, and met with the landlady's instant approval when I offered to take her Scottie dog for walks. I thought Blackpool was a fascinating place – a huge fairground built on golden sands. It has one of the finest beaches in the country; and something I had never seen before – young women riding horses, very odd indeed. Where I lived, horses pulled carts, and ploughs and milk-floats, but here, they chased up and down the wet sands when the tide was out, ridden by excited girls (never any boys). I asked Aunt Janet, whose sour-faced reply was, "Rich lasses. Nowt better to do," and we left it at that. I had enough money for a donkey ride, but knew it would have been "too bumpy".

So, in the long hours when Aunt Janet was working and I had to amuse myself, I wandered about the foreshore, watching the mill-workers of Lancashire enjoying themselves; they were simple pleasures, sitting in the sun in deck-chairs, paddling, eating ice-cream, fish and chips from newspaper, cockles, whelks and pikelets. There were "amusement arcades" full of flashing lights and machines designed to gobble up your spending money – not many prizes. I remember standing watching the lifts going up and down The Tower, that remarkable structure, only a pale shadow of the Eiffel, but it stood looking out on this maelstrom of colourful, hectic activity, all day and into its flood-lit night, which I was not allowed to experience. I would have loved to go to the circus, but anything which cost more than a penny was out. And for a penny, a child could go on the pier, and I did, every day. The end of the pier, windy and foam-soaked, was the next best thing to an ocean liner in the middle of the Atlantic. And there were concert parties singing our favourite tunes – you didn't have to pay and go inside, you could hear quite well on a bench outside.

One early evening after tea, one of the paying guests came in roaring drunk, and I was bundled upstairs, smartish, but I could look out through the tiny dormer window and watch the lights coming on; – even in early summer, the town was full of coloured lights, not at all like our village. When the landlady's husband told me that Blackpool was the first town in the WORLD to be lit by electricity, I thought he was pulling my leg, but I've since discovered it was true. And that's why there are the illuminations every autumn, bigger and better and brasher. I went home by myself on a coach, care of the driver; in those days it was possible, for a small fee, to send parcels, children, grannies, watched over, hopefully, by a kindly man at the wheel.

There was hardly any traffic. I felt VERY grown-up, and had embarked on my long career of people-watching; it was a successful baptism, and is an activity I still unashamedly pursue.

I went back to school in the new term in September, and found the daily routine very irksome. I'd enjoyed a free-wheeling life for eight months, and I would have liked it to continue. Somewhere about Christmas, I learned that being in hospital had not meant the end of "the scholarship", and I was to be allowed to take it in February,. "Not a hope," I decided, "all that missed school." But I passed, as did a boy from the same class, and the arguments started. Would it mean bus fares, school uniforms, how much, how much? Our neighbours were keen to point out that education was wasted on a girl – "they only get married." My cousin, Jean, always held up as a glorious shining example, was, at 14, already learning shorthand-typing, and "would get good money in a couple of years."

Because we lived 200 yards outside the city boundary, Sheffield schools were not an option and the place offered was in a newly-built, 5-year-old, grammar school at Ecclesfield, half-way between Sheffield and Barnsley in the West Riding, seventeen miles away. Best forget it. But mother had other ideas. She went to see Mr. Heeley and learned that there was a special bus collecting children from the country villages, absolutely free; I would be first on at 7.30am, and last off at 5pm. And because I was exempt from all sports and P.E., there would be no expensive equipment to buy – just a gym slip and blazer; mother could make the rest. It was decided, with the proviso that if it "didn't work out", I could leave at fourteen and go into an office. Oh! it HAD to work out! Please, it had to. Grandma made disapproving noises – to which I was completely deaf.

Ecclesfield was an expanding village in mining country, its ancient origins completely obliterated by Newton Chambers' vast chemical works, which made, among other things, the very popular disinfectant IZAL, whose pungent odour permeated the entire neighbourhood. The school was a great surprise – stone-built, two storeys, huge windows, glass-roofed corridors, with an enormous central hall, classrooms on the ground floor, science labs and art rooms upstairs. The whole building was surrounded by tennis courts and playing fields which covered acres. But the biggest surprise came on the first morning when I presented my medical certificate to the Headmaster, Mr Arthur Harrison. He informed me that pupils excused games and P.E. must spend these periods in the library! Library? Schools had libraries? I had never been in one, and it was vast; hundreds of books, on floor-to-ceiling shelves, they could be read in situ, and borrowed to take home. Wonderful... !

The school was co-ed, and the staff also mixed gender. There was a headmistress as well as a headmaster, and with the exception of the science teachers, they all wore black gowns! Echoes of public school sounded everywhere. Four houses, Harrow's school song ("Forty Years On"), full morning assembly. The Annual Speech Day took place in the Miner's Hall in Chapeltown, and prizes were delivered by Lady Mabel Smith, a local grandee whose family wealth issued from way underground, and was black. Most of the pupils were the sons and daughters of miners, factory and railway workers (from villages with exotic names like Jump, Wombwell), and were there courtesy of scholarships, like myself. Some were fee-payers, and could always be recognised by their posh, leather satchels – offspring of shop-keepers, school teachers and other professionals, but we all wore the same disguise in the school colours – parsley, beetroot and egg. Gym-slips were green, blazers maroon and badges yellow. The boys sported grey flannels and we all wore ties. The prospectus had informed us there was a school shop where second hand uniforms could be purchased half-price, and there I was kitted out in great hand-me-down tradition. I was very careful where I wore this camouflage – certainly not in the village of Stannington, but as I passed through each day in a 'luxury coach', the problem did not arise. Five country villages in reservoir terrain provided our passengers, who stood, like ducks out of water, in all weathers, awaiting our arrival. The journey to school took one-and-a-half hours, with a return after 4pm of the same time.

The first games period found me in the library, sharing a table with a brown-haired girl who was frantically sketching in a rough book. We were both obviously over-awed by our new situation, and there was no conversation until I asked why she was excused games. She bent down, picked up a stick from the floor, and lurched across to the bookshelves dragging a withered leg in an iron calliper. She came back, sat down, grinning. "Polio when I was six." she said. We never mentioned it again.

My generation's early years were over-shadowed by the 1914-18 war (The Great War). It had scarred the lives of our parents; there was an overwhelming sadness, so many widows, so many women who never married, so many fatherless children. And hard on its heels came the polio epidemic, to add to the number of damaged bodies hobbling on crutches.

We met four or five times a week in the library, allies in adversity, but cheerfully recognising that we hated organised games of any kind, and succeeded in the next five years to avoid contact with any hockey-stick, tennis racquet or vaulting horse. We would look out of the library windows and feel truly sorry for the poor sods chasing around in the mud, thwacking balls and winning trophies. My new friend's name was Joan Clarke – the second J. Clarke of that unforgettable time. "Can't do anything but draw," she said, and it was true. Academic subjects were not her forte – 10% for maths, "must try harder" for everything else but art. Everybody knew she was headed for Art School, and being a fee-payer, she was not going to be thrown out of Ecclesfield Grammar School.

And I had begun to eat my way through all those books, high brow and low brow, Kierkegaard to P.G. Wodehouse. I would masticate anything in print for a year or two, and then preferences reared their heads. We had a wonderful English teacher called Alfred Jowett – a young man, prematurely grey, who always wore lurid-coloured socks hand-knitted by his mother, and a gown already in tatters, that he clasped to his bosom every few minutes. He had an infectious grin, and loved satire. I became a disciple, a swot, a new term to me, with connotations not exactly endearing, but I cared not. Our A-Form did Latin and we were each given a French correspondent. Mine was called Olga Labinsky, and lived in Casablanca, and we wrote letters to each other regularly. Joan coaxed me into the Architecture class, which gave me a life-long pleasure in buildings, but my efforts at drama were short-lived and doomed to failure – I couldn't bear the exposure. I was 15 before I entered a theatre, and I started at the top – the Shakespeare Memorial Theatre at Stratford. Brain-child of the head of English, Mr. Clay (who collected weekly subs of two shillings from pupils interested), the annual camp shone bright in the firmament of extra-mural activities. We slept six to a bell-tent, and went to the theatre every evening; Shakespeare was not something we read in books – Shakespeare was LIVE, with famous actors of the day

– Donald Wolfit, Rosalind Iden, John Mills, Peggy Ashcroft among them. We spent most afternoons larking on the river in rowing boats and punts; the mornings exploring the town, the highways and byways (especially the byways), the secret gardens, the ancient buildings, with a member of staff whose enthusiasm was infectious. Every evening we went to the theatre, cheapest seats of course, but that was of no consequence. One performance of Macbeth we sat through, blissfully unaware that a thunderstorm was raging outside. When we reached the camp-site we found it was completely flooded – everything we had was waterlogged, tents, bedding, clothes, food, there was no sleep that night, and the drying-out operations went on for days.

After the theatre, there was always a post-mortem with the bed-time cocoa, and the most effusive, intelligent and passionate contributions came from a boy 2 or 3 years my senior. His father was the station-master at Ecclesfield – he was the star of the school drama club, shining brightly in every production, and we knew he would be an actor. He was conscripted into the RAF straight from school, went to RADA after the war, and became ultimately a very famous film-star, specialising in baddie roles. His name was Donald Pleasence. I went to three Stratford camps and probably saw every Shakespeare play ever produced.

But back to the piano. During my six months of convalescence, I drove the family to distraction with my front-room sessions of hymns and pop songs, all in one key, with a squeaking pedal. Mother became ambitious for me, and announced one day, "No child of mine is going to be a domestic servant," and decided I should have some music lessons, – cheap. Cousin Conrad's young lady Ida had passed several music exams, and was taking on Saturday pupils at 6d a time. I was enrolled, and as soon as I could walk again, I embarked on the mysteries of black dots, bar lines, time signatures and clefs. Ida frowned on my Charlie Kunz ambitions, and set me off on the straight and narrow with Czerny exercises, scales and simple classical pieces. But I still "ear-wigged" from the wireless, and have always loved the romantic songs of my youth – Irving Berlin, George Gershwin, Cole Porter.

After about 18 months, the weekly lessons ended. I expect the money ran out, but I kept on playing, not with any great ambition, but for pure enjoyment, and when the Sunday School accompanist became ill, I took on playing for the hymns. I have played for singers ever since. I could (and can) keep very strict tempo and improvise – small talents, but before the days of tapes and CDs, very useful assets. When I was 14, I acquired a Saturday afternoon job, playing for a dancing school in Pitsmoor, three hours' playing for the handsome sum of two shillings, which now sounds miniscule, but two shillings went a long way in 1936 – a piece of music, a Penguin paperback, some knitting wool, and later, a cinema seat and some chocolate. I was referred to as "Miss Helliwell" always, and given grown-up status; I was most likely being shamefully exploited, but it never occurred to me that I was anything but extremely fortunate. I enjoyed it enormously.

My brother won a Scholarship to the Technical College, and our lives diverged even further. I was an enthusiastic Girl Guide, but loathed the uniform. I became leader of the Kingfisher patrol, and won badges for cookery, embroidery, "entertainer", and goodness knows what. But I had no friends in the village, and there was no social life that I would even consider. School was the place for that, with my ally and confederate, my disabled friend Joan, who aided and abetted me in enterprises mad and bizarre. We decided that if we made overtures to certain prefects (weekly chocolate bar usually proved an excellent tune), we could occupy the library in the lunch hour. We wrote stories which Joan illustrated with her wicked, satirical pen, launched a monthly magazine, which fell by the wayside because we had neither typewriter nor access to a duplicator, and we read and read the books around us. It's difficult to believe now that duplicating was such a complicated procedure, but in the 1930's there was very little technology available. We rarely met out of school – it meant buses and trams, going through the city, which was too difficult for Joan; it was expensive for me to visit HER and her parents were not exactly welcoming – thought I was a bad influence, living in No-Man's land, with a father who mended cars. Le Père Clarke had some exalted position in one of Sheffield's steel works, and dressed at Jaeger – a fact which did not escape his daughter's scathing pen. Our greatest scorn was poured on loud-mouths, show-offs, "look-at-me" people, fashion, cosmetics, and humbug in all its manifestations. Pretentiousness of ANY sort, we could not abide. We were full-steam-ahead for trouble; and we ARGUED. Some teachers encouraged this and others put us down – but they couldn't ignore the fact that, athletics apart, we won laurels. Joan made off with the annual art prize, and I won the form prize for general studies, every year.

Homework escalated. There was only one table in the house, where all food was prepared and eaten, and I usually found myself writing on a cramped corner of this whilst meals were going on and the wireless was merrily playing. In grandma's bedroom there was no space for even a card table, and we were now the proud owners of a dilapidated 3 piece suite, whose vast bulk occupied the whole of the front room, which was rarely used except for piano practice. And it was COLD. Never mind.

There were school trips to London, Edinburgh, Paris, Switzerland, but they were all far too expensive for our meagre income. I was more than happy to be able to go to the Stratford Summer camp. It was the highlight of my year, and I couldn't believe my good fortune, to be a small part of such excellence, in such exotic, cosmopolitan surroundings. In the queues and on the streets, we spoke to people from all over the world – I saw my first Chinese people there (they probably lived in London), chatted to Americans; there were no foreigners on the streets of Sheffield and certainly no black faces.

It was long before the days of screaming fans, but when we stood patiently waiting for autographs, I was a FAN, of Shakespeare first and the actors second, and every time we rowed or punted past the red-brick Art-Deco theatre, we saluted, in all earnestness. To a child growing up in a country village in the shadow of Steel Metropolis, Stratford was a revelation, my first acquaintance with the cultured life and a yardstick for all future experiences. One sunny afternoon, lying idly in a punt tethered to a green willow, I knew that I had fallen in love with the Avon, and I made a solemn vow that one day I would live next to a river. It took twenty years, but it happened.

I had by this time discovered the Big City. My Saturday afternoon job, playing for 'tap', ballet, and 'modern', in a dusty church hall in Pitsmoor led me to the edge of the vast, urban sprawl, and, my pockets bulging with all of two shillings, a tram ride brought me to city centre commerce, the High Street emporiums, markets, cutlery workshops, warehouses, Central Library, the theatres and cinemas. There was much exploring to be done, hours of people-watching to indulge in.

The REAL core of Sheffield, its raison-d'être, the source of its great wealth and world-wide fame, lay in the east end with its giant steel works, dozens of tall chimneys belching out black, sulphurous smoke on to the surrounding mean streets where the sun never penetrated, where it was a waste of time to hang out washing, and where its stinking, effluent-laden rivers had not harboured a fish since before the Industrial Revolution. The workers laboured in round-the-clock shifts, in cruel temperatures, clad only in boots, trousers, and sweat-rags, tending the furnaces, the crucibles, and working the machines which fashioned everything from cutlery and small tools to all-steel armour plate for battleships. The four largest firms specialised in the armament industry, making guns, gun parts and projectiles, shells and ammunition, and the four miles between the city centre and Rotherham had the greatest concentration of heavy industry in the world.

Sadly, Joyce's memoir ends here, abruptly and cruelly interrupted by the death of the friend who was helping her to put it together.

Joyce Kitching: A sketch of a life

Joyce went on to become a teacher. While employed at Bennet College, a correspondence college in Sheffield, around the outbreak of the Second World War, she met an artist, Arthur Kitching, also teaching there. In 1946 they were married, and she moved into another crowded Sheffield two-up-two-down not far away, and not so very different from, the one described so vividly in her memoir. This they shared with Arthur's mother, brother, sister-in-law, sister, and niece. But they escaped at weekends to a caravan in one of the Derbyshire villages. They also began holidays on the Continent, on a financial shoestring but rich in art and experience.

In 1950 they finally made a break from Sheffield, and went to live in Essex, first in a caravan in Burnham-on-Crouch and then in a rented bungalow in Chelmsford. Their first child was born there. Eight years after the escape south, they moved back north, to another part of Yorkshire. The house was a huge, dilapidated Victorian building which Joyce's father had been unable to sell, in a fabulous location overlooking a bend in the river Wharfe, in Ilkley. This was when, as Joyce had promised herself twenty years before, she got to live beside a river. Their second child was born shortly after.

Joyce never again moved from the Ilkley riverside. After Arthur retired, they moved a short way along (but still within sight of) the river, to a smaller terraced house. Arthur sadly died in 1981, shortly after the move.

Both the Ilkley houses were places of gathering, of holidays, of bases for walking the moors and the dales, of refuge, of short- or long-term accommodation, for many people – two children and their spouses, four grandchildren, and many other friends and relatives (if the people who took rented accommodation with them were not already friends, they soon became so).

Joyce died in 2010. She had touched so many lives.

Printed in Great Britain
by Amazon.co.uk, Ltd.,
Marston Gate.